I0454121

COZY COLORING & DRAWING

BOBBIE GOODS

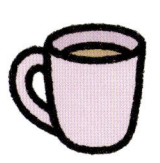   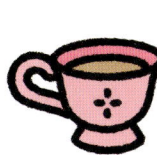 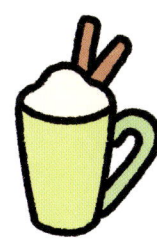

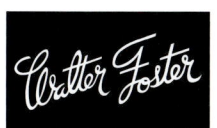
Walter Foster

Quarto.com | WalterFoster.com

© 2026 Quarto Publishing
Text & Illustrations © 2026 Bobbie Goods

First Published in 2026 by Walter Foster Publishing, an imprint of The Quarto Group,
100 Cummings Center, Suite 265-D, Beverly, MA 01915, USA.
T (978) 282-9590 F (978) 283-2742

EEA Representation, WTS Tax d.o.o.,
Žanova ulica 3, 4000 Kranj, Slovenia.
www.wts-tax.si

All rights reserved. No part of this book may be reproduced in any form without written permission of the copyright owners. All images in this book have been reproduced with the knowledge and prior consent of the artists concerned, and no responsibility is accepted by producer, publisher, or printer for any infringement of copyright or otherwise, arising from the contents of this publication. Every effort has been made to ensure that credits accurately comply with information supplied. We apologize for any inaccuracies that may have occurred and will resolve inaccurate or missing information in a subsequent reprinting of the book.

Walter Foster Publishing titles are also available at discount for retail, wholesale, promotional, and bulk purchase. For details, contact the Special Sales Manager by email at specialsales@quarto.com or by mail at The Quarto Group, Attn: Special Sales Manager, 100 Cummings Center, Suite 265-D, Beverly, MA 01915, USA.

30 29 28 27 26   1 2 3 4 5

ISBN: 978-0-7603-9846-3

Digital edition published in 2026
eISBN: 978-0-7603-9847-0

Printed in Guangdong, China TT062025

contents

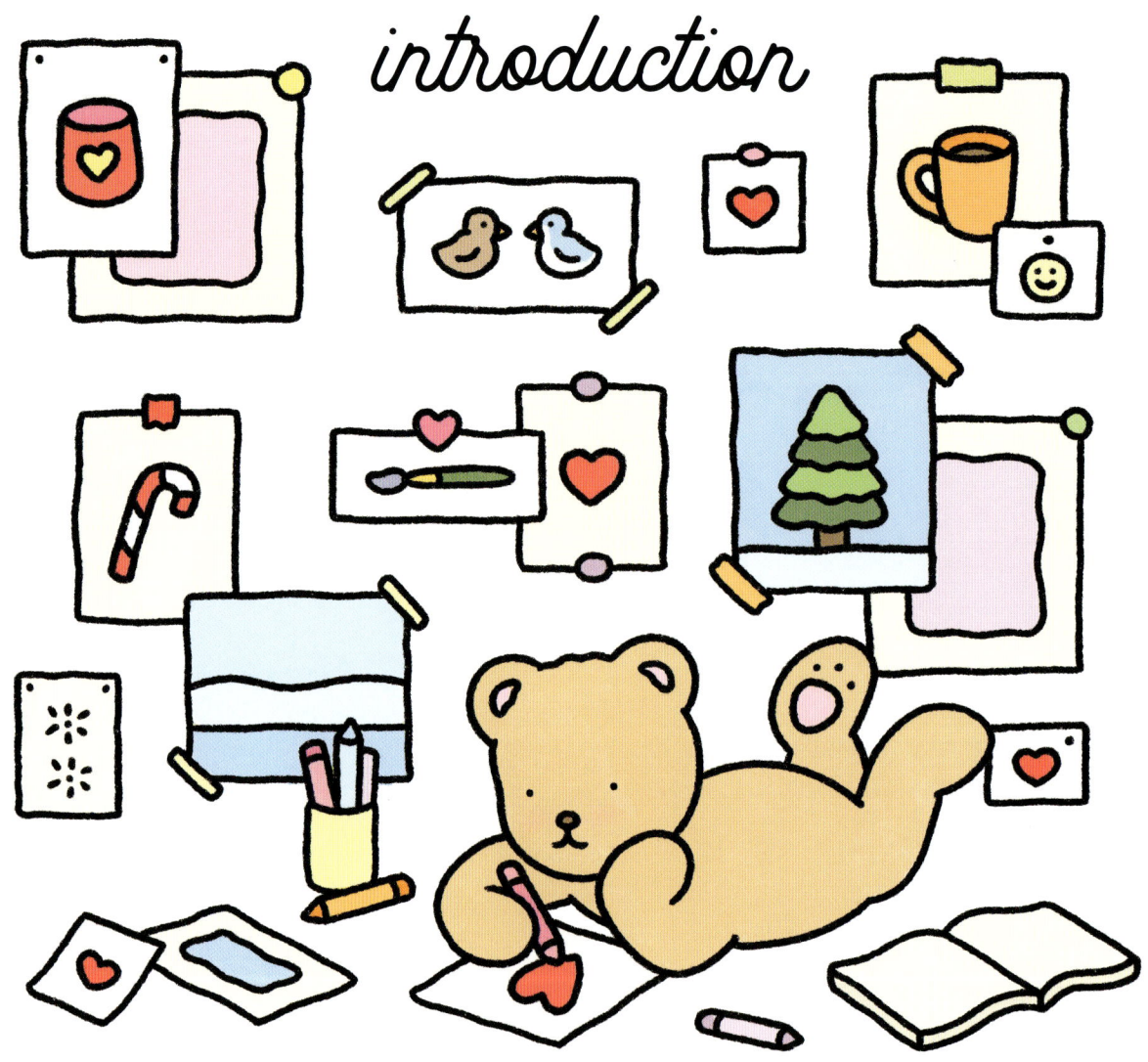

introduction

Bobbie Goods is a world that's full of quirky characters living out their adorable daily lives. Delightfully nostalgic, Bobbie Goods brings comfort to people of all ages.

Get cozy and grab a pen or marker to draw your own adorable world. Fill it with delightful characters like puppies and bears, scenes like cozy cafés and snowy days, and fun holiday decor. This book also comes with an attached pad featuring coloring pages and memo sheets perfect for jotting down notes, practicing your drawings, or sending a letter to a friend! Whether you're relaxing by the fire or looking for a creative holiday activity, Bobbie Goods offers a delightful, hands-on way to enjoy the season.

tools & materials

You don't need anything fancy to get started; simply choose supplies that you're comfortable with and that you'll enjoy using. Here are a few suggestions to kick off your coloring and drawing journey:

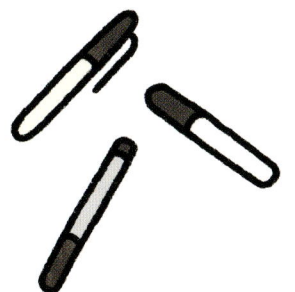

Black Pen or Marker: Choose your favorite black pen or marker as your primary tool for creating the bold contour lines that Bobbie Goods is known for! Even though you might make mistakes at first, practicing with a dark pen can help you develop your own style and a precise hand. The more you do it, the better you'll get!

Paper: This book includes a fun pad of coloring pages and memo sheets, along with a handy flap to place between pages to protect against your markers bleeding through. Use the memo sheets for drawing, making lists, or even sending notes to friends!

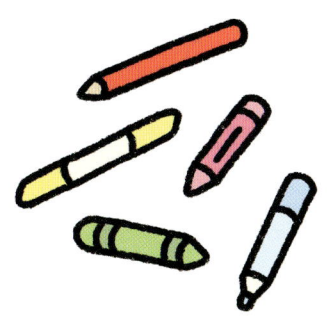

All Your Favorite Colors: Choose the medium you prefer, whether it be markers, colored pencils, or crayons, to bring your drawings to life with vibrant hues. It can help to pick your favorite colors and then shades in between to give your masterpieces more depth and pop!

drawing techniques

Don't worry if your hand isn't perfectly steady! Wiggly, imperfect lines add extra personality to your drawing. In fact, Bobbie never uses perfectly straight lines in her drawings!

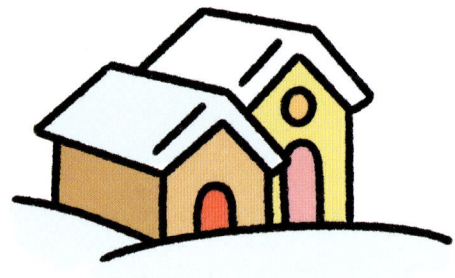 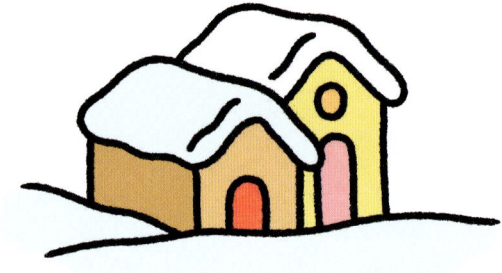

These houses are pretty nice. . .   but *these* houses are one of a kind!

When drawing Bobbie Goods characters, think about how changing an outline to make a dog extra shaggy or silky smooth can give them a whole new look.

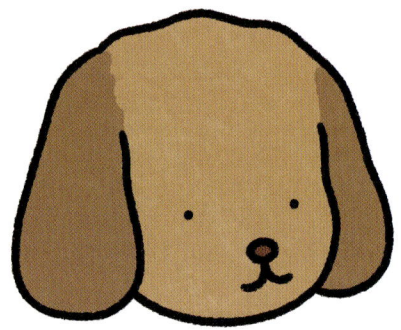 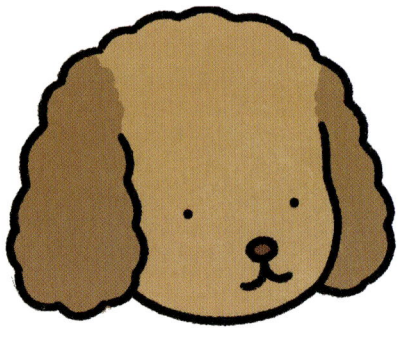

This puppy is sleek and shiny!   This puppy is perfectly puffy!

characters

Here are some friendly faces from the world of Bobbie Goods! Do you recognize them? Who's your favorite character?

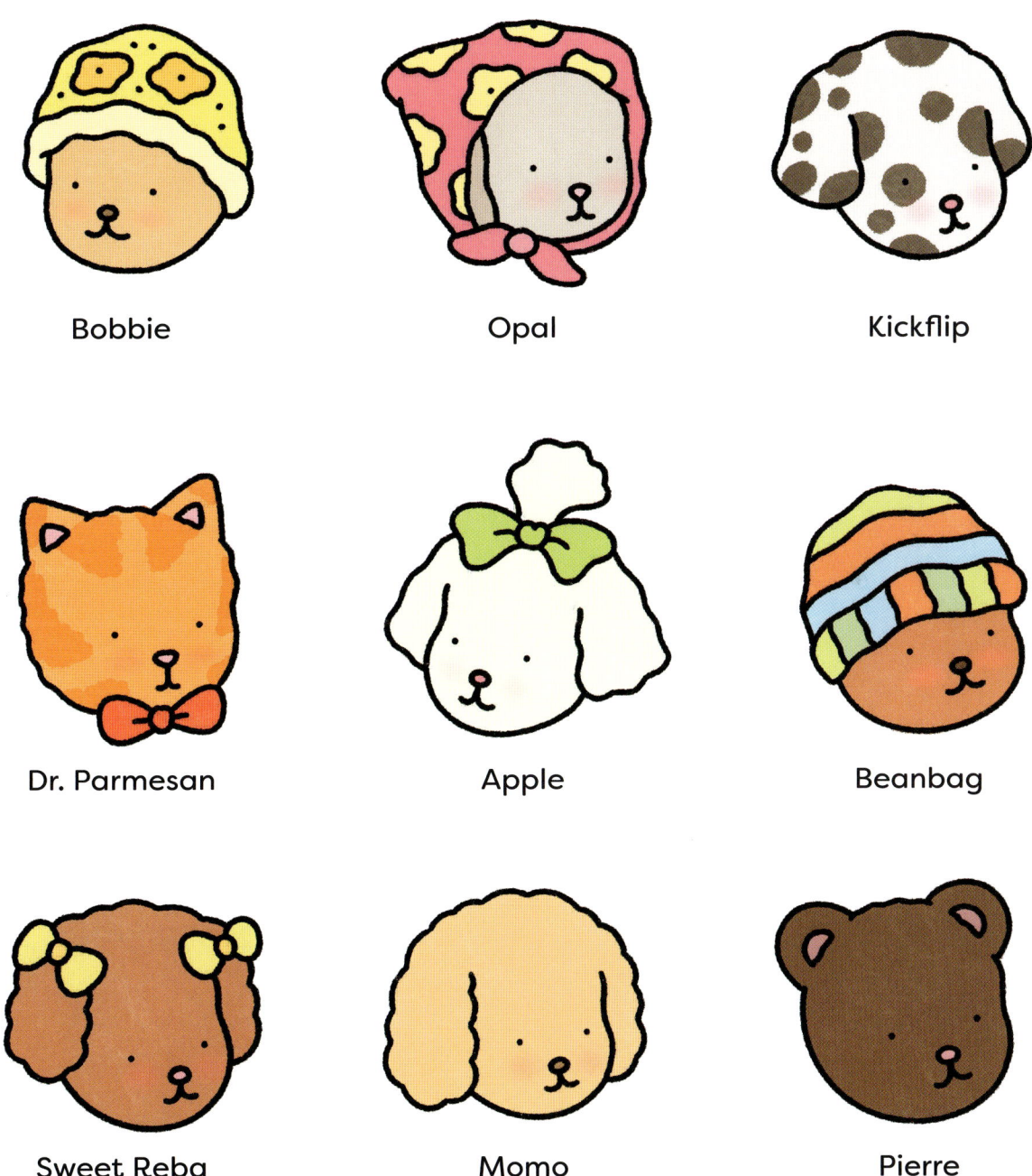

Bobbie

Opal

Kickflip

Dr. Parmesan

Apple

Beanbag

Sweet Reba

Momo

Pierre

HOT COCOA CAFÉ

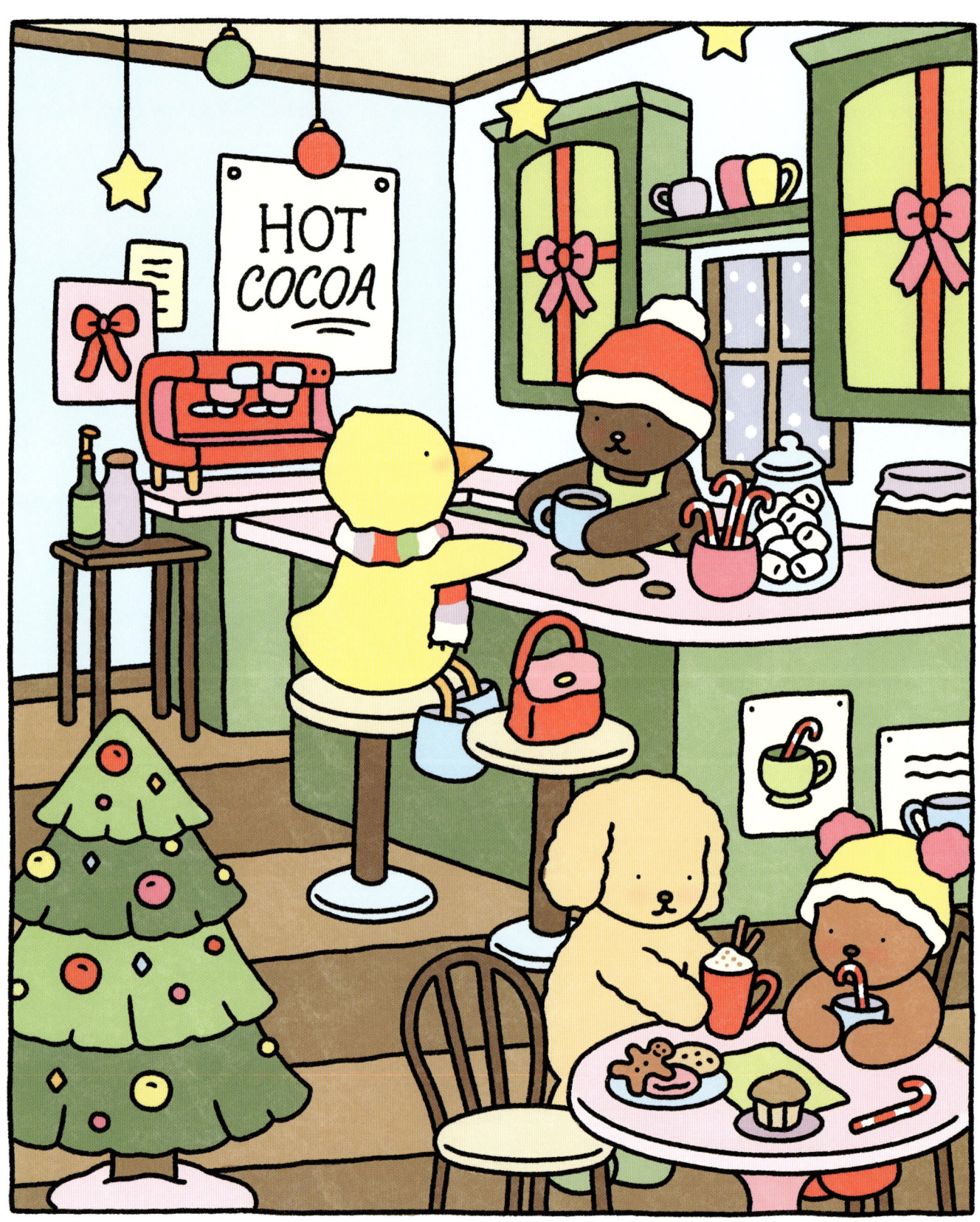

plate of cookies

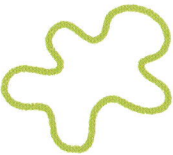

 Start with a squiggly gingerbread cookie shape.

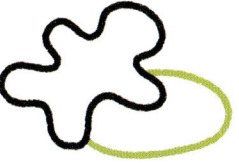

 Next add the first round cookie.

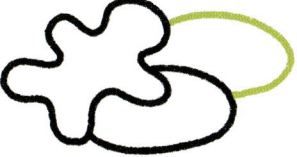

 Add another cookie under the gingerbread.

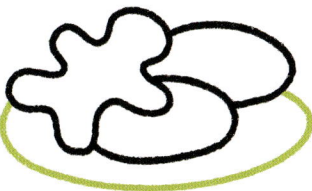

 Then draw a half oval for the plate.

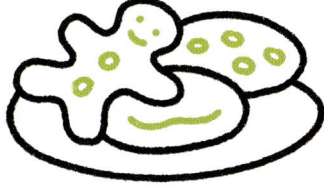

 Add a face and buttons to the gingerbread and any other decorations for your cookies. Yum.

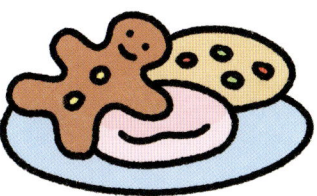

 Choose colors for the cookies and frosting.

decorative tree

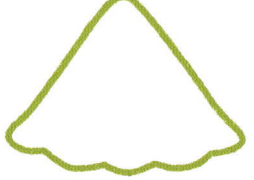

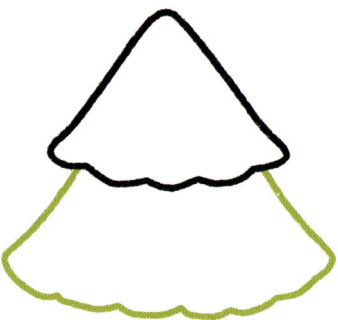

 1 Start by drawing the top of the tree with a rounded point and a wiggly bottom.

 2 Next add the second layer. Make sure it's a little wider than the first.

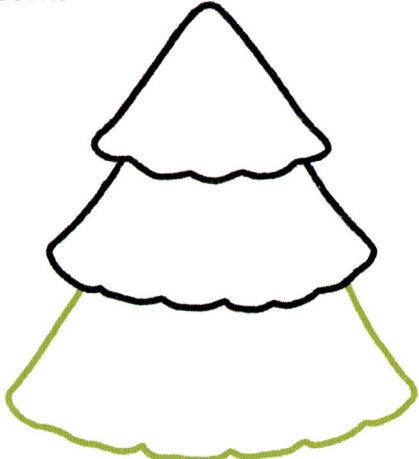

 3 Now it's time for the third layer. Make it even wider.

 4 Add the fourth and final layer.

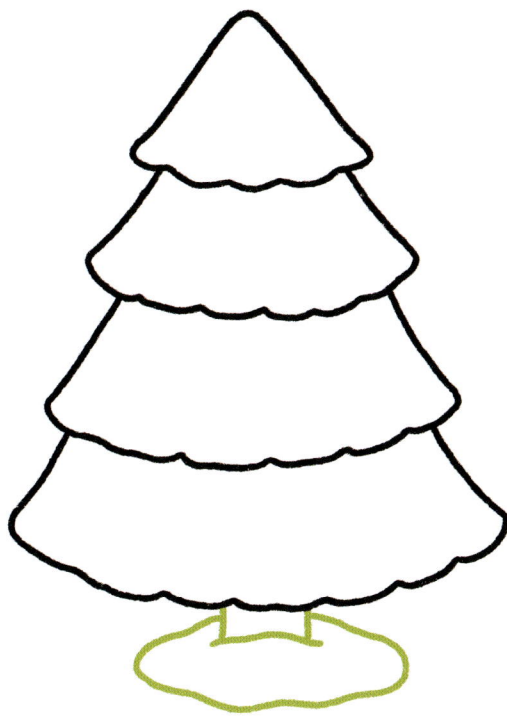

 It's time to add the trunk of the tree and a little tree skirt.

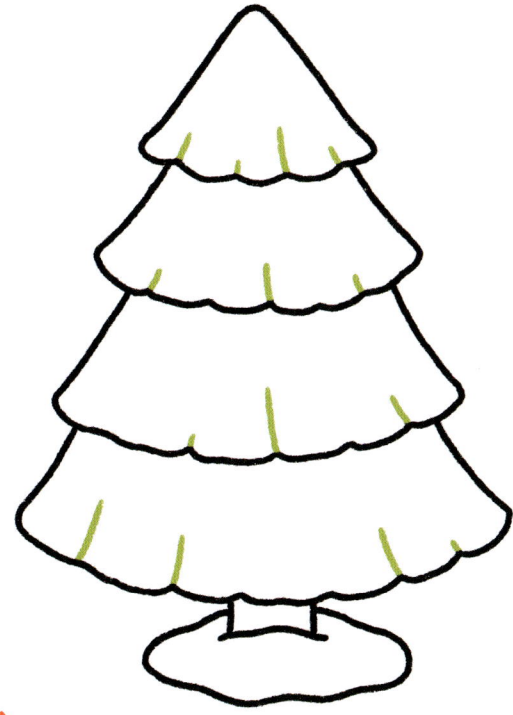

6 To give the tree a little dimension, add some lines at various heights.

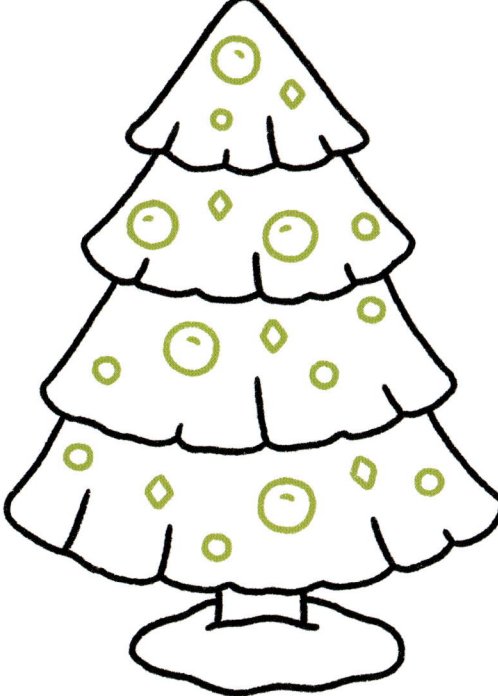

 Next add some fun ornaments. So festive!

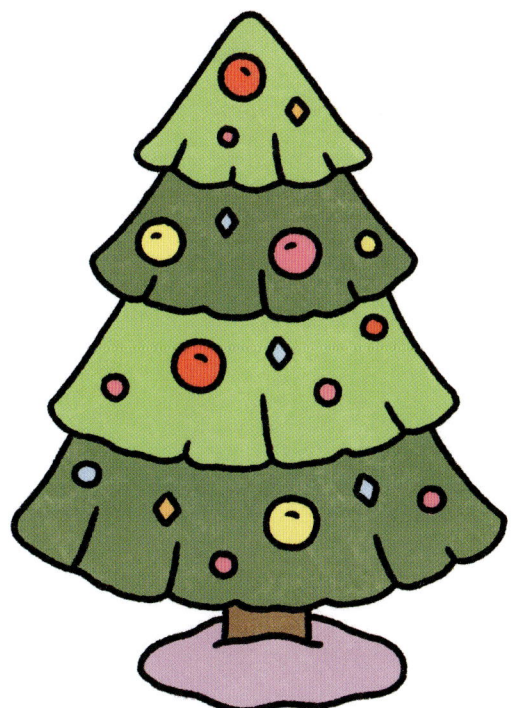

 Finish with your favorite colors.

hot cocoa

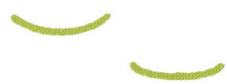

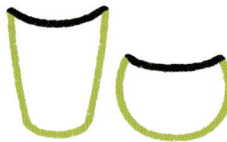

 1 Draw two small curved lines next to each other, one lower than the other.

 2 Add the bottoms of the mugs. The shorter one will be more rounded.

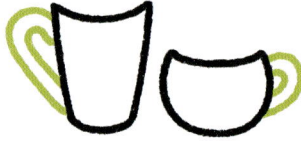

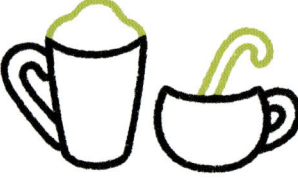

 3 Draw two lines like half of a heart to make the handles for each mug.

4 Draw a squiggly line for whipped cream on the tall cup and a candy cane in the small mug!

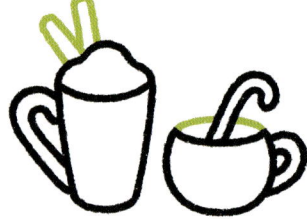

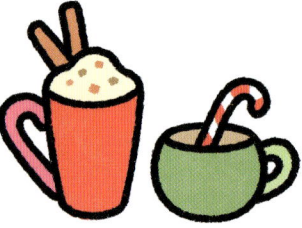

 5 Add two stick shapes to the whipped cream and a half oval to finish the small mug.

 6 Choose your colors and decorate!

12

THE PERFECT TREE

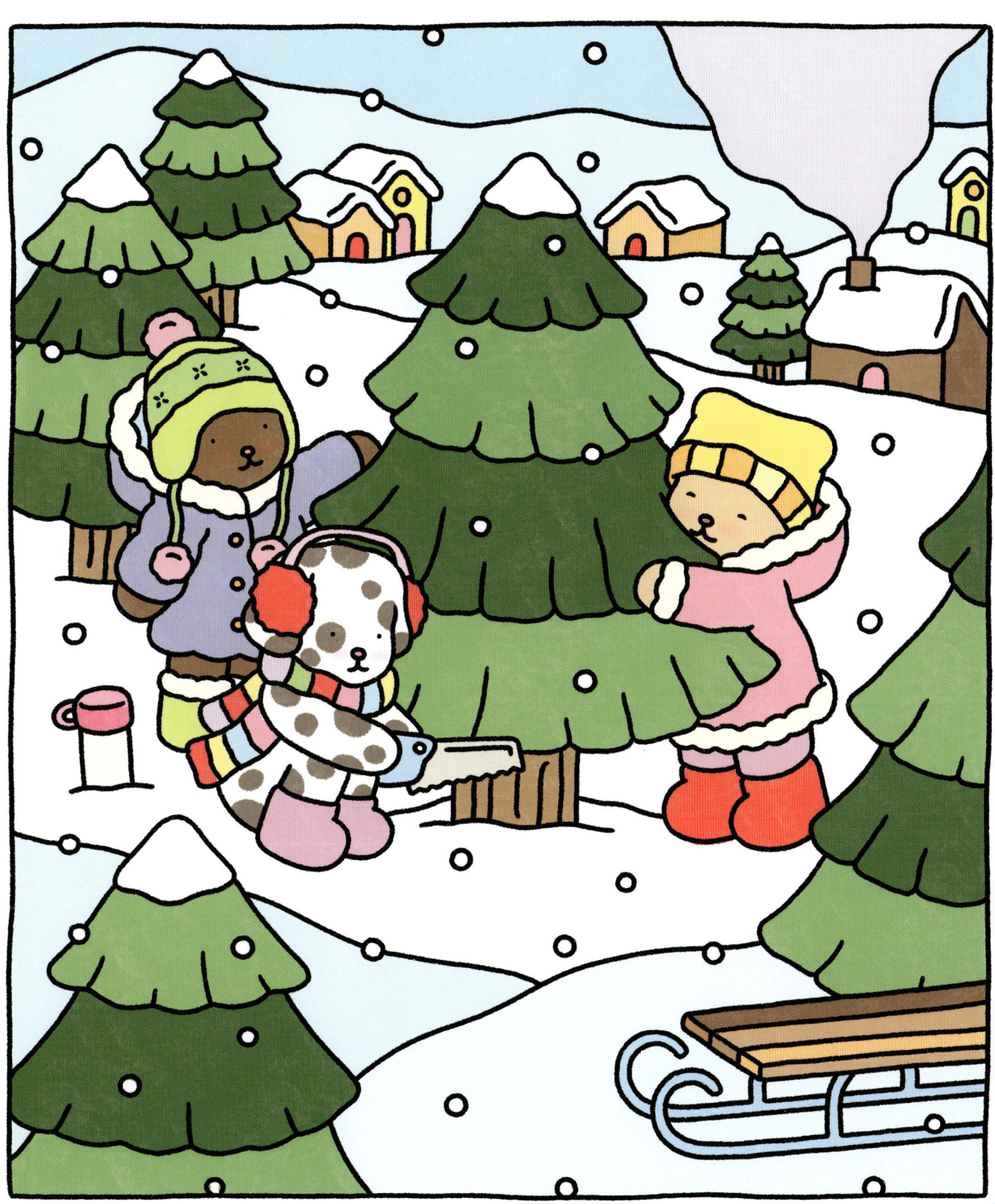

sled

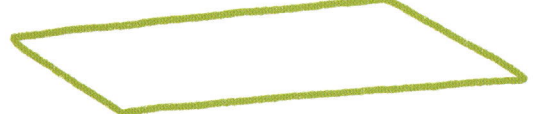

 Draw a slanted rectangle. This will be the seat of your sled.

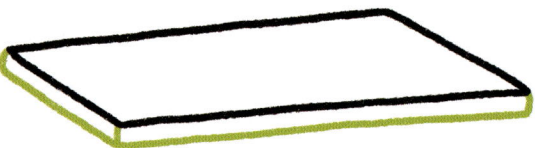

 Add three tiny lines and connect them to give the sled some depth.

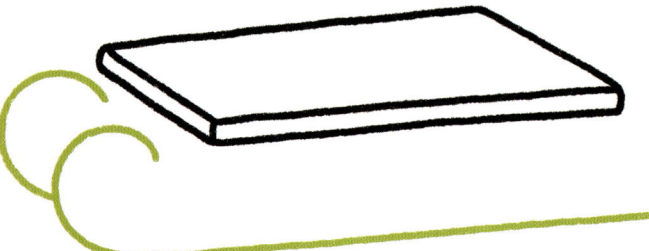

 Draw a C with a very long tail for the sled runner. Add another C without a tail.

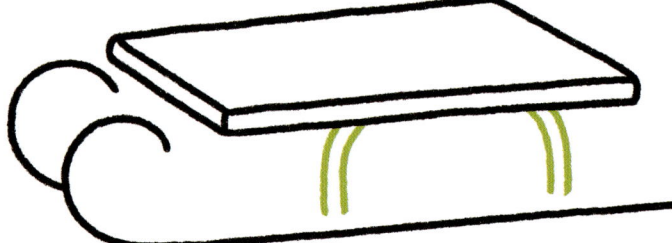

 Add four curvy vertical lines.

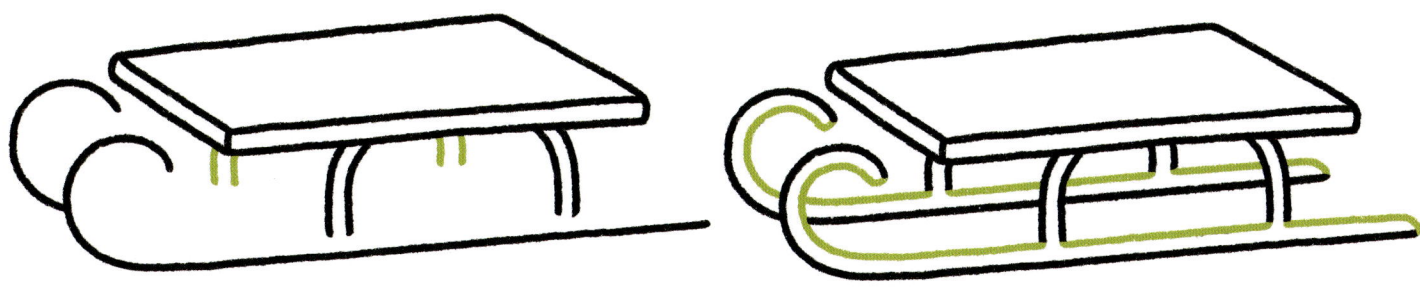

 And four more tiny lines on the other side of the sled.

 Connect the runners to the seat like this.

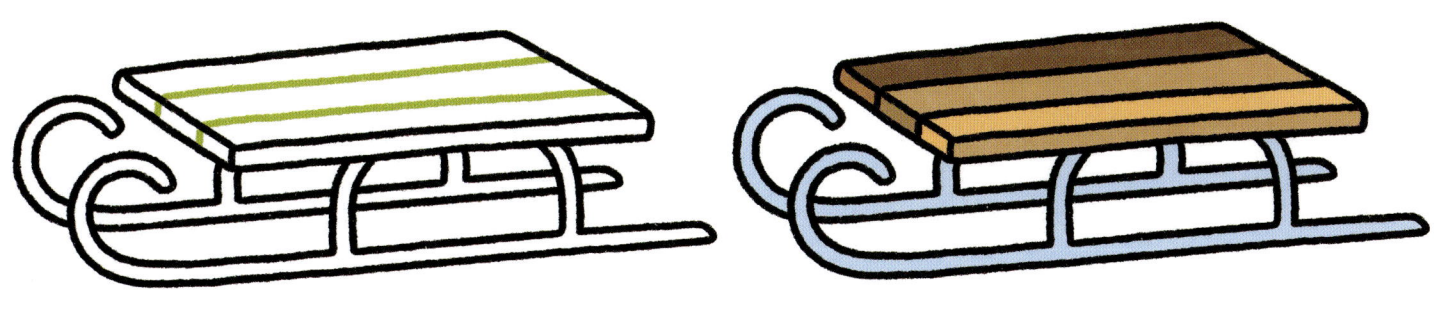

 Add some lines. Wow, it's wooden!

 Choose your colors.

snowy houses

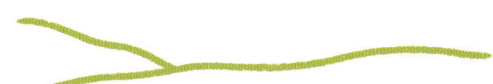

 Draw two squiggly lines for your snowy landscape.

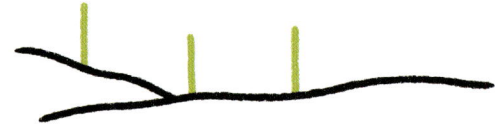

 Add three lines to make your first house.

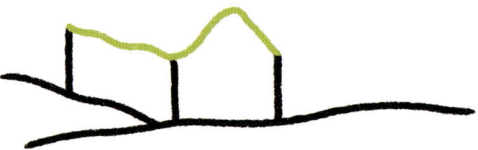

 Add a squiggly roof. The front will angle up in a rounded point.

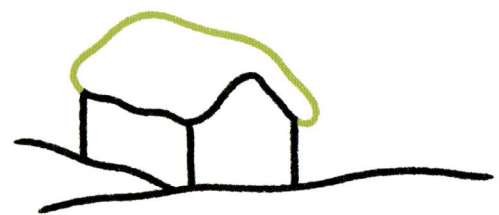

 Now add the thick snow on the roof. It's sticking!

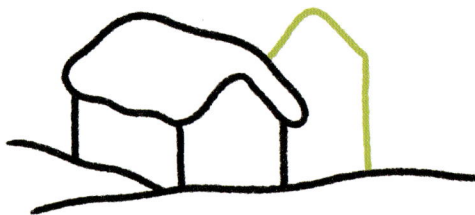

 Add another house next door.

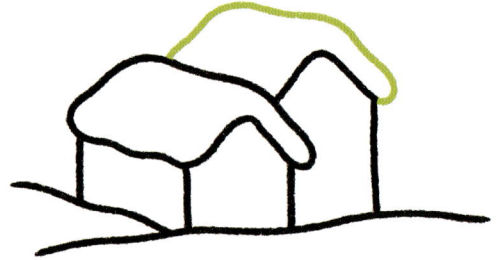

 Draw another squiggly roof.

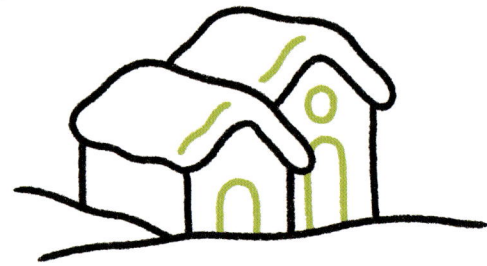

 Add the details to the houses.

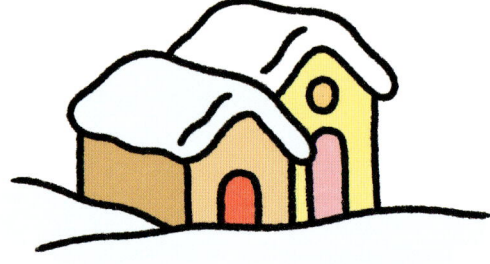

 Color your cozy cottages! Brr, it's cold outside.

pom-pom beanie bear

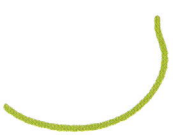

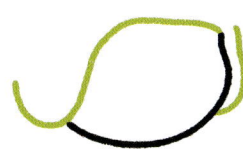

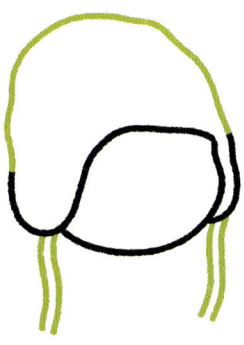

1 Draw a curved line for the bear's face.

2 Add two more curvy lines. These will be the cute ear flaps.

3 Connect the ear flaps to make the hat. Draw two strings coming down from each ear flap.

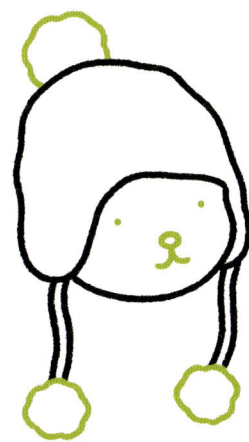

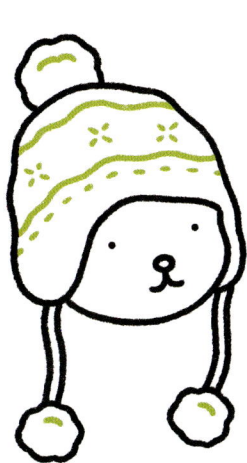

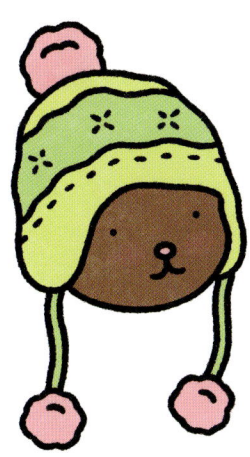

4 Add a puffball to the strings and one on top of the hat. Draw a cute face for your bear too!

5 Design your hat any way you like. Add little squiqqles to show how fluffy the pom-poms are.

6 Color your pom-pom beanie bear!

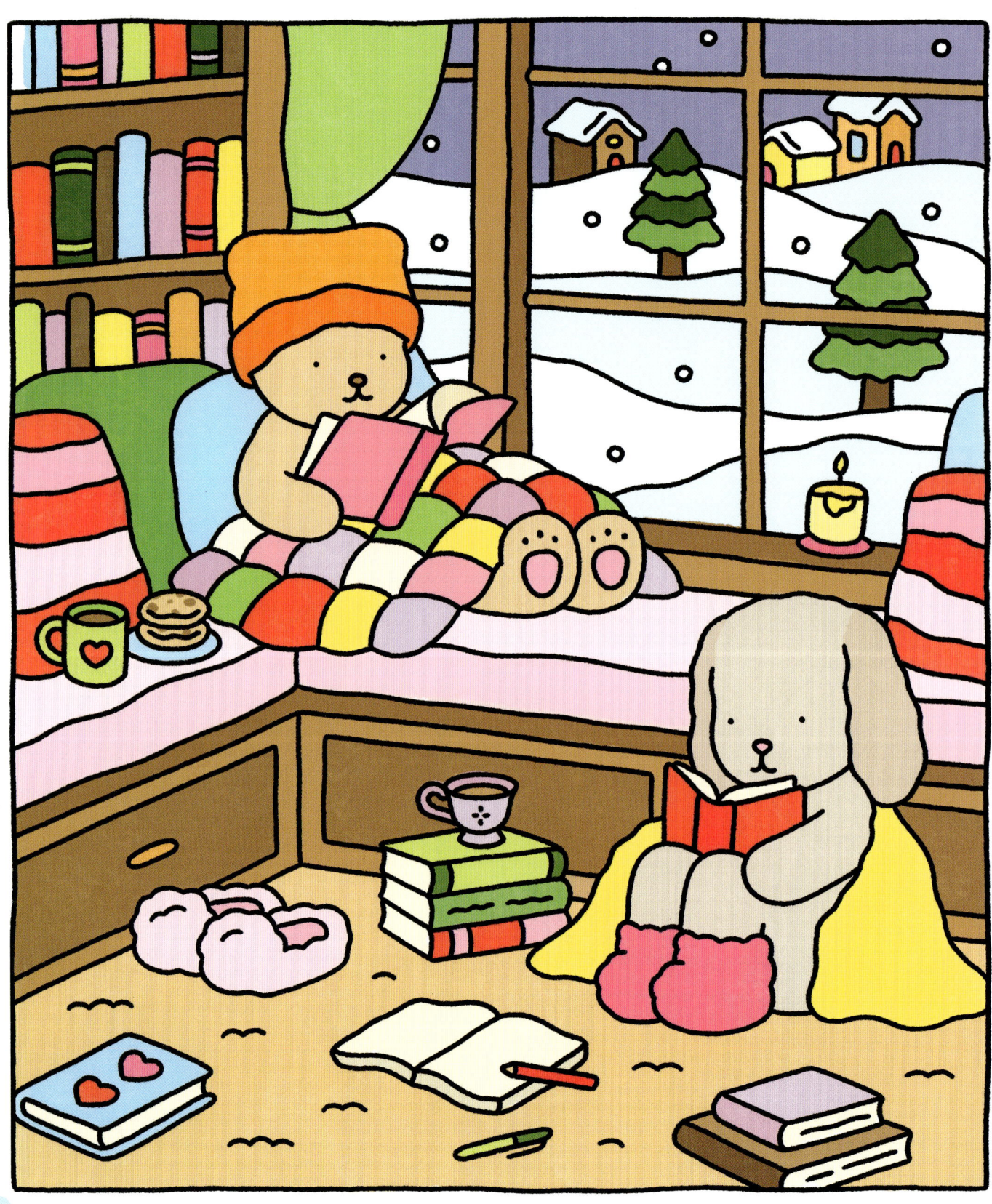

fuzzy slippers

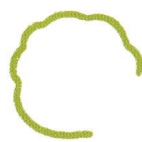

 1 Draw an almost-finished puffball.

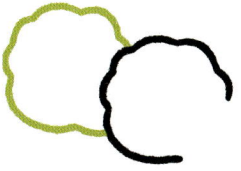

 2 Add another almost-finished puffball next to the first.

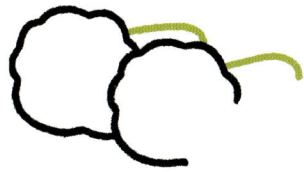

 3 Draw two short, curved lines coming out of the puffballs.

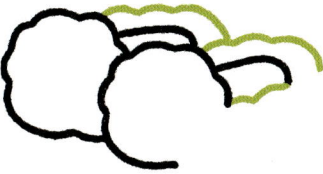

 4 Add squiggly lines curving around the other lines.

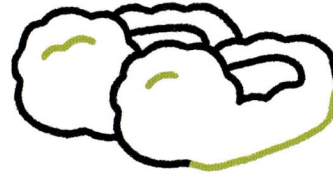

 5 Connect all the squiggly lines to make the slippers. So fluffy!

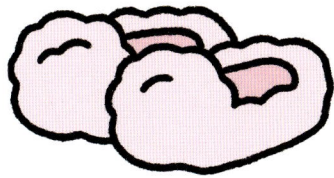

 6 Choose a color for your new fuzzy slippers.

stack of books

 Draw four parallel lines.

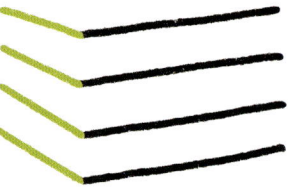

 Add four more slanted straight lines that connect to the first.

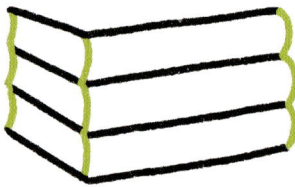

 Connect the ends with curved lines for the edges of the books.

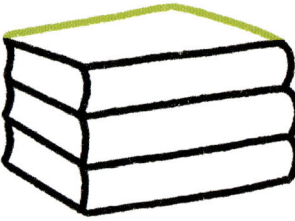

 Finish the top book by adding the cover.

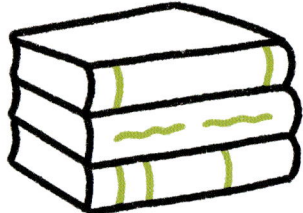

 Add detailing on the spines of the books. Cool!

 Color the books. Bobbie and Opal love to read!

beanie bear

 1 Draw a rounded line.

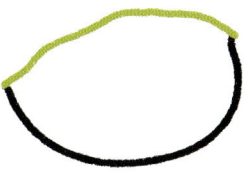

 2 Add a squiggly line on top.

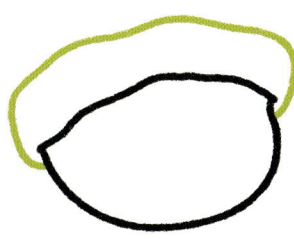

 3 Make another slightly wider squiggly line.

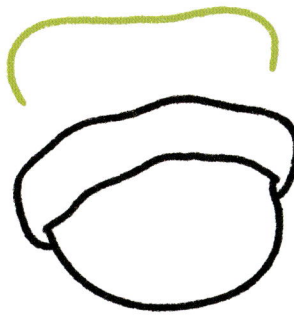

 4 Add a line for the top of the hat, but don't connect it yet.

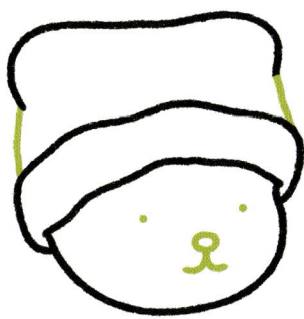

 5 Now connect the lines to make the hat. Add a sweet bear face as well. Cute!

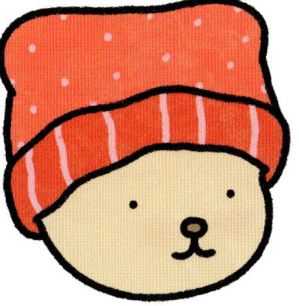

 6 Add whichever colors you think suits this bear best.

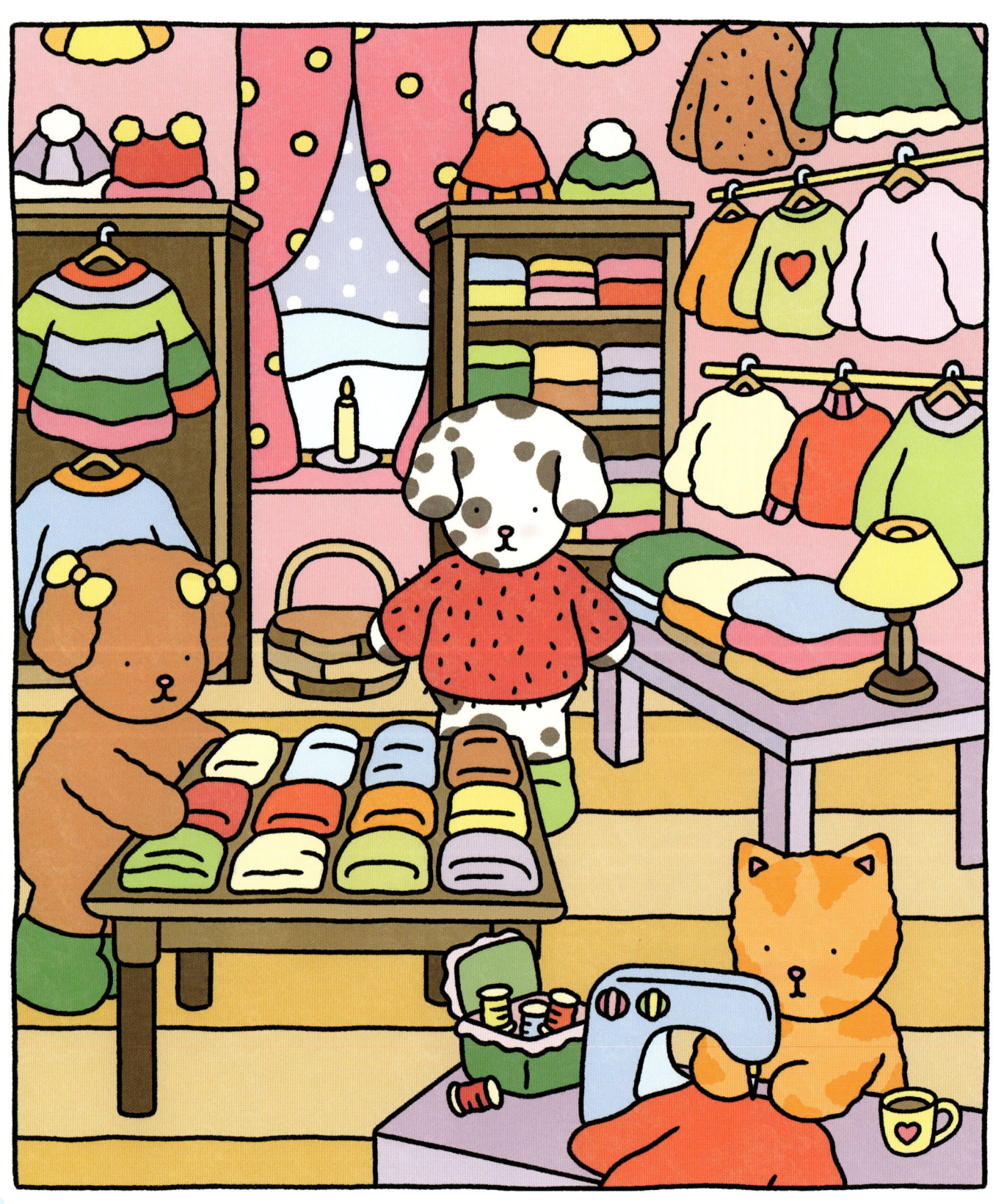

sewing machine

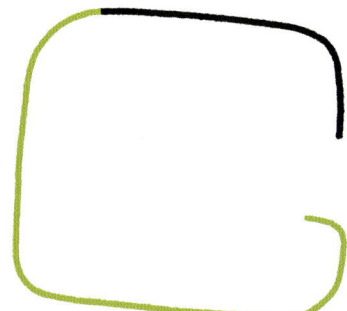

 1 Make a long, curved line. This is the top of the sewing machine.

 2 Add the other half of the curved line.

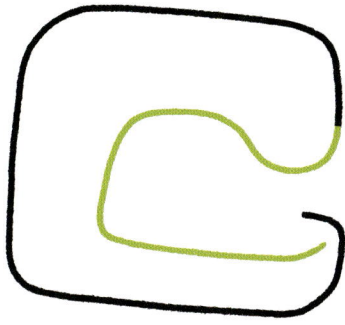

 **3** Draw a curvy line with a gap.

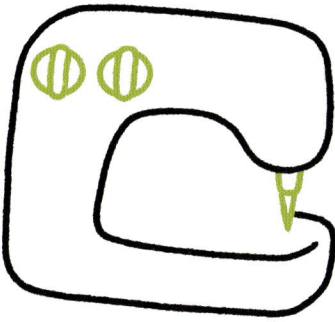 **4** Add the knobs and needle. Almost time to sew!

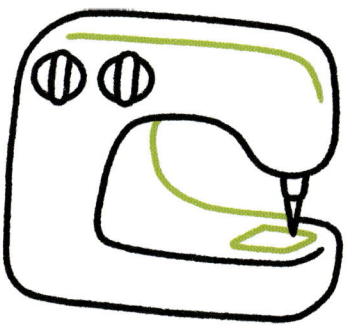

 5 Draw more curvy lines and a tilted square under the needle.

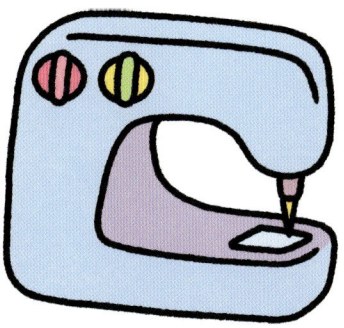 **6** Choose colors for your new sewing machine!

sweater puppy

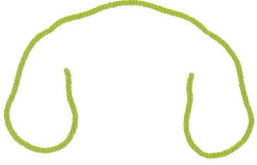

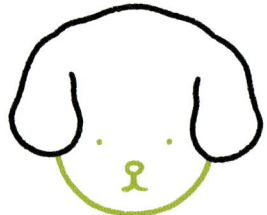

 1 Draw squiggly lines for the dog's floppy ears and top of its head.

 2 Add the dog's chin and a shy face.

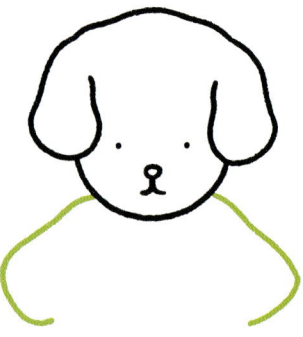

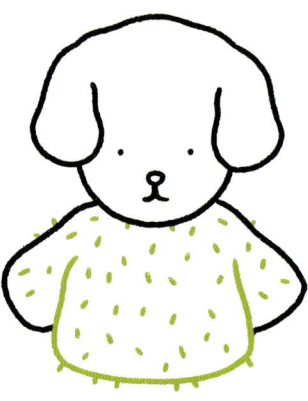

 3 Draw some angled lines for the sweater sleeves.

 4 Make a big U shape for the bottom of the sweater and add fluffiness!

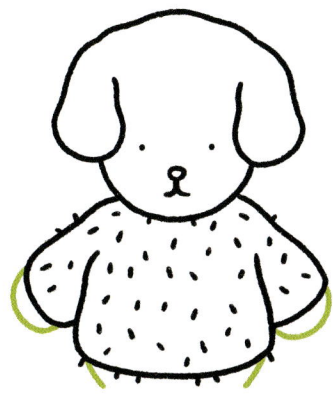

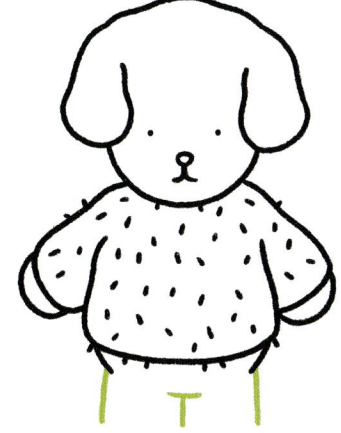

5 Add little half circles at the end of each sleeve for the puppy's paws. Draw two angled lines for the start of the legs.

6 Make a T for the center of the legs and add two parallel lines.

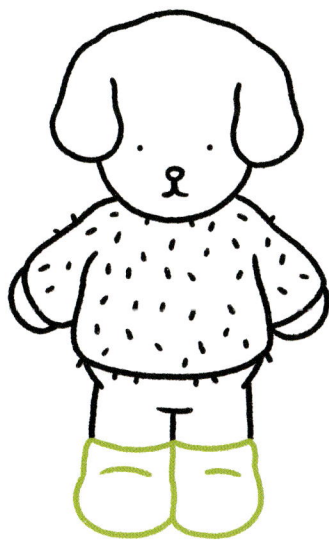

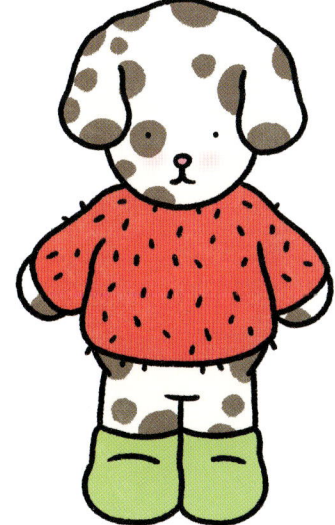

7 Add boots! Cute!

8 Color your cozy pup!

striped sweater

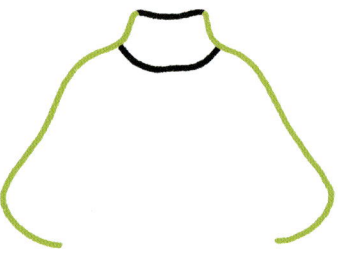

1 Draw two curved lines.

2 Add the outline of the arms.

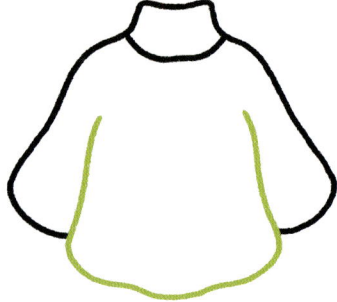

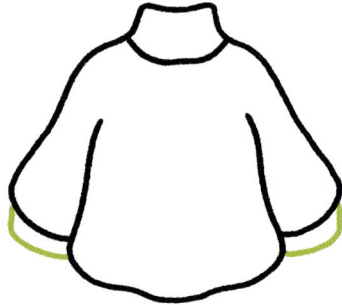

3 Make a squiggly U shape for the bottom of the sweater.

4 Add two curved lines for the sweater cuffs.

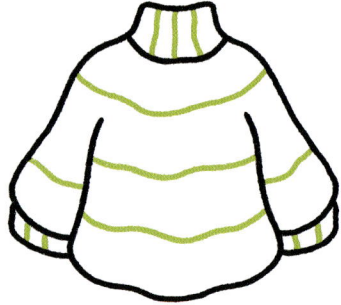

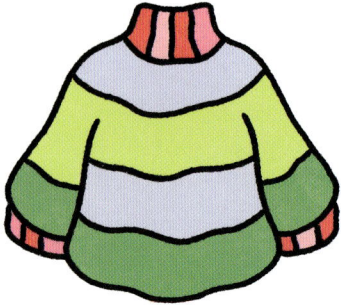

5 Draw stripes and lines for the turtleneck and cuffs!

6 Choose your favorite colors for your cozy sweater!

SNOW CONE STAND

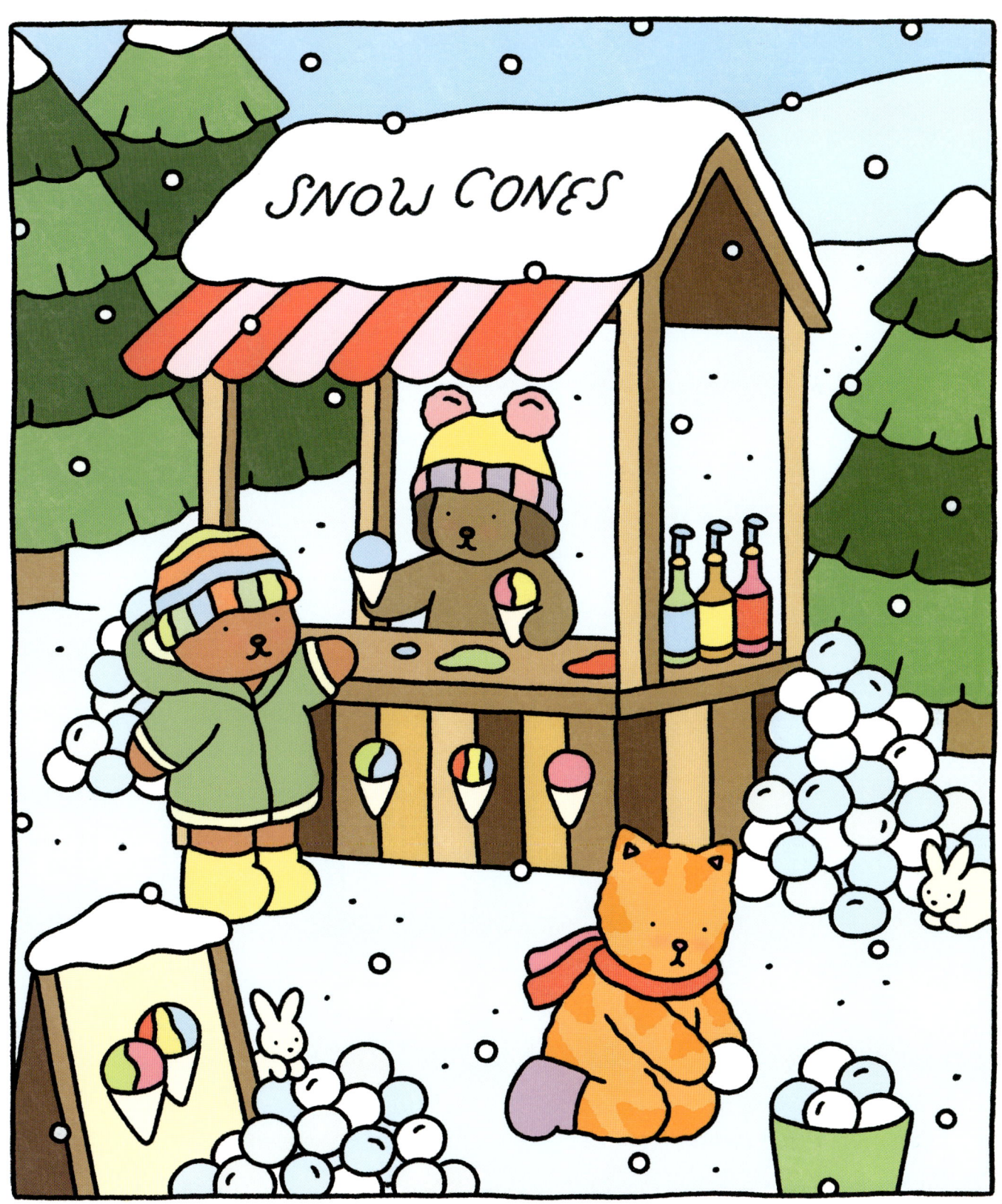

market stand

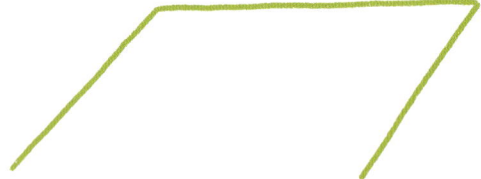

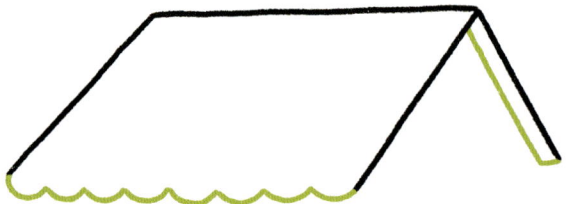

 Draw a tilted unfinished rectangle to start the roof.

 Add a scalloped edge and lines for the back of the roof.

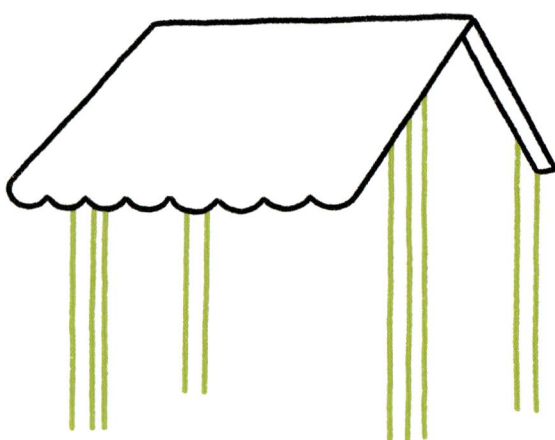

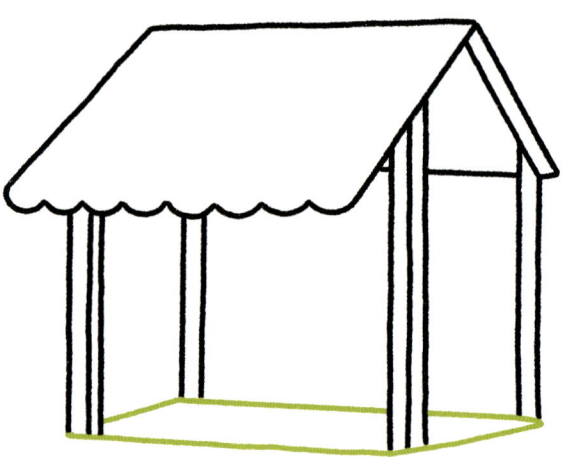

 Draw lines going down from the roof for the poles of the stand.

 Add the stand's counter.

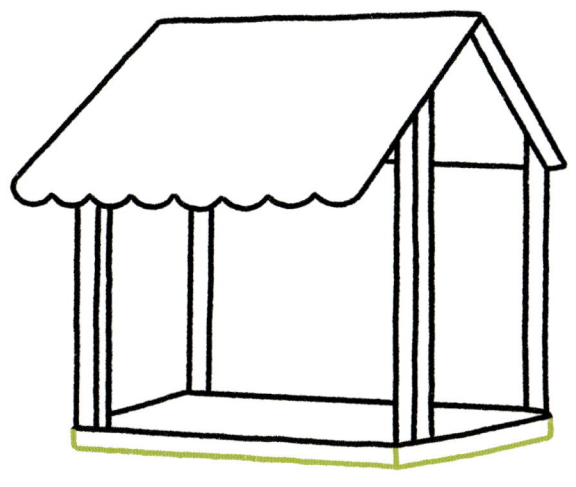

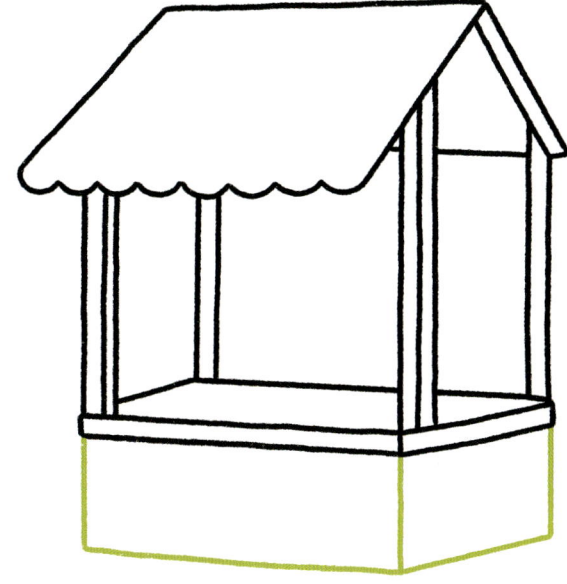

 Finish the counter.

 Add the base of the stand.

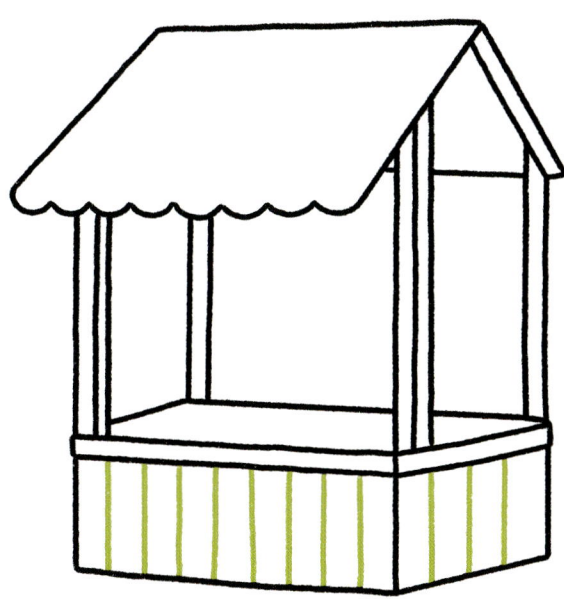

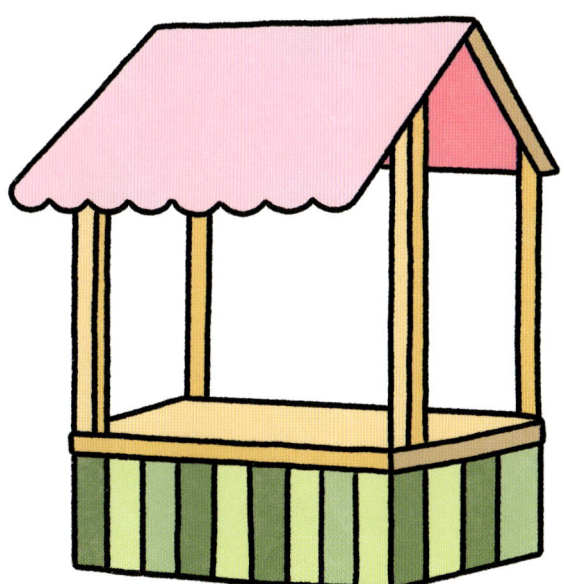

 Draw some lines for the boards!

 Fill it with colors that pop!

snow cone bear

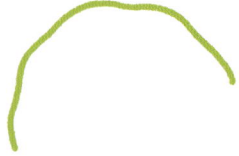

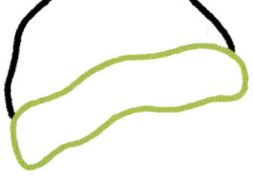

 1 Draw a squiggly line for the top of the hat.

 **2** Add squiggly lines to connect the base of the hat.

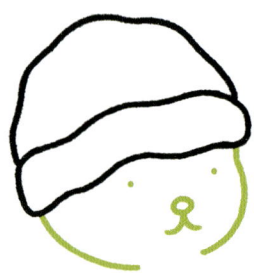

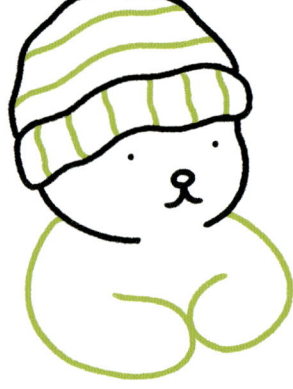

 3 Draw a cute little bear face!

4 Draw some curved lines for the arms and paws. Add some lines for the hat design!

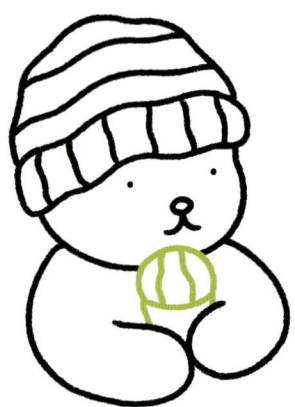

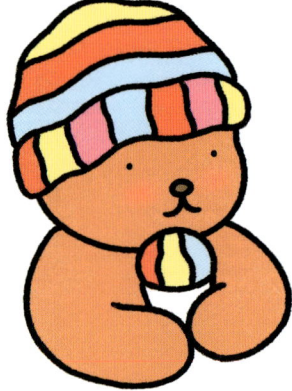

 5 Add the snow cone in the center of the bear's paws.

6 Pick your favorite colors.

snow cones

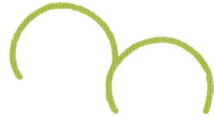

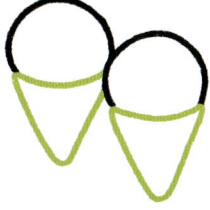

 Draw two half circles next to each other.

 Add triangle shapes for the cones!

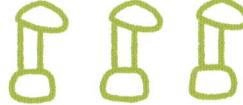

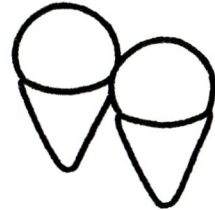

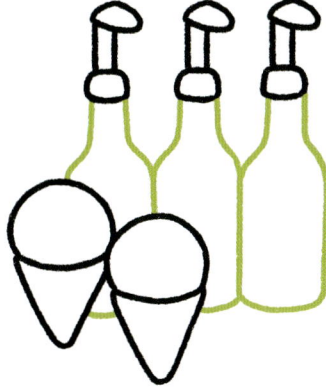

 Next draw the tops of flavor pumps.

 Draw three bottles connected to the pumps. What flavors are they?

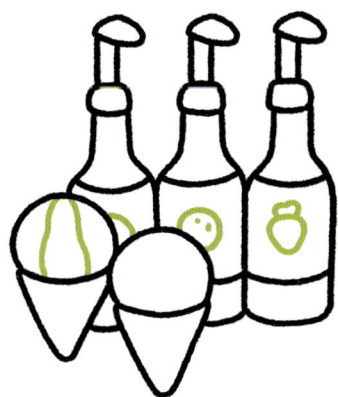

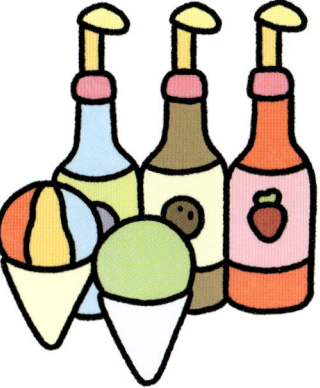

 Add details for the flavors and snow cones! Yum!

 Color and enjoy the yummy treats!

about the artist

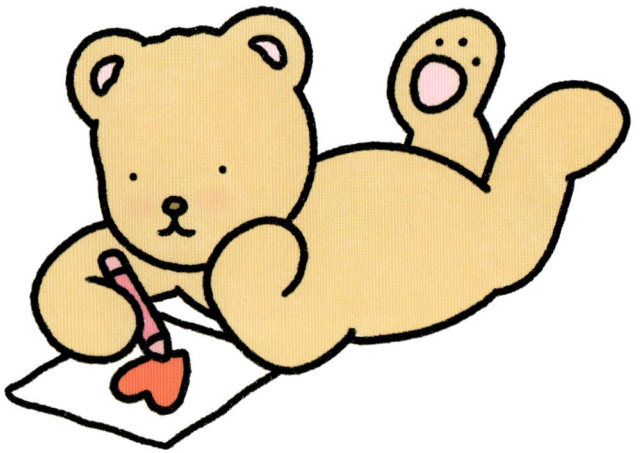

Bobbie Goods was created by Abbie "Bobbie" Goveia in sunny Southern California. Bobbie is an artist and designer who started drawing at a very young age, and she hasn't stopped since! Through her drawings, Bobbie strives to convey an appreciation for nature, kindness to others, and comforting nostalgia. Bobbie Goods is a source of creativity and connection for people all around the globe . . . including you!

Discover the world of Bobbie Goods in her many coloring book editions, or you can follow along with her drawing process, step by step, in *How to Draw Super Cute Things with Bobbie Goods*. Find out more at bobbiegoods.com.

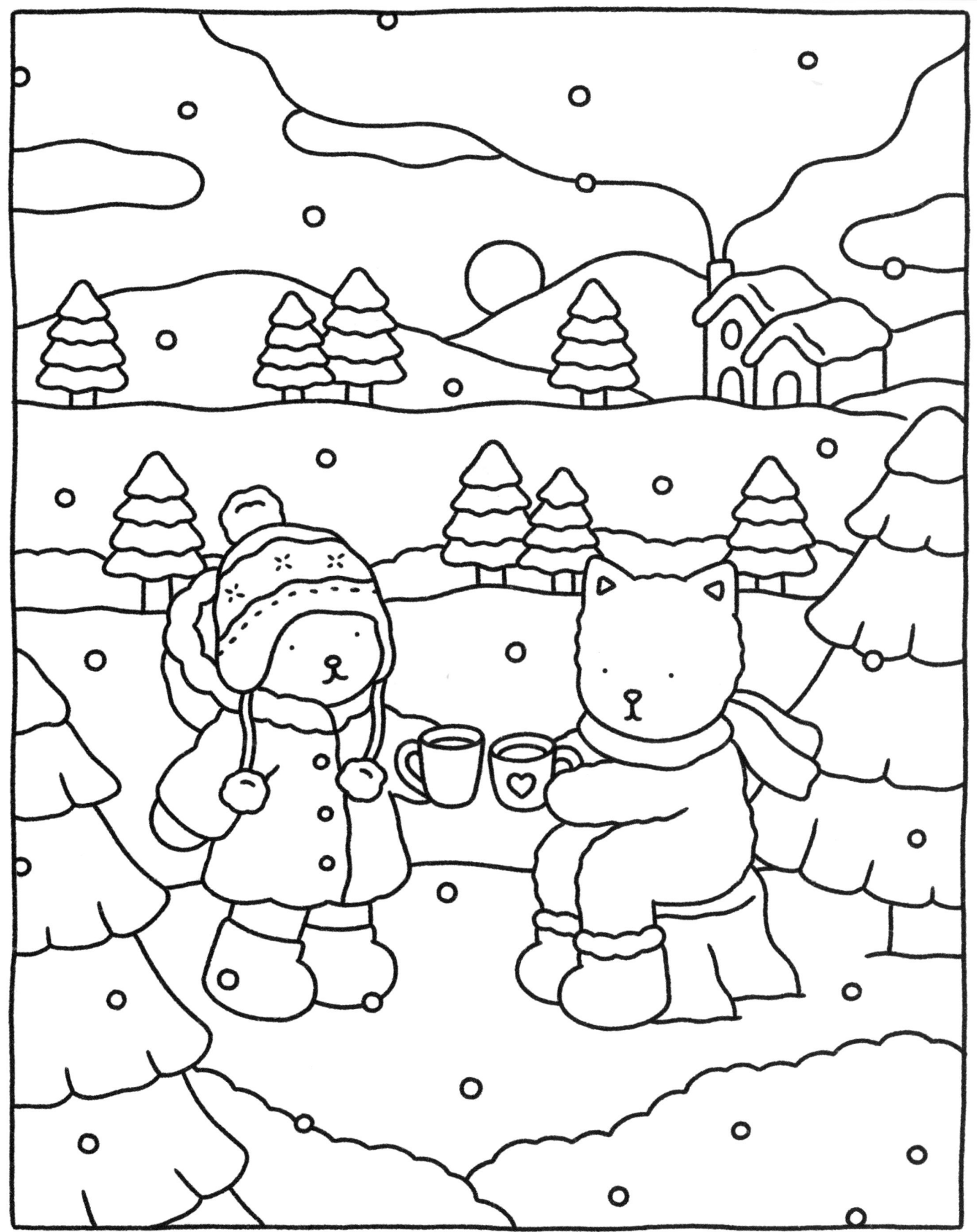

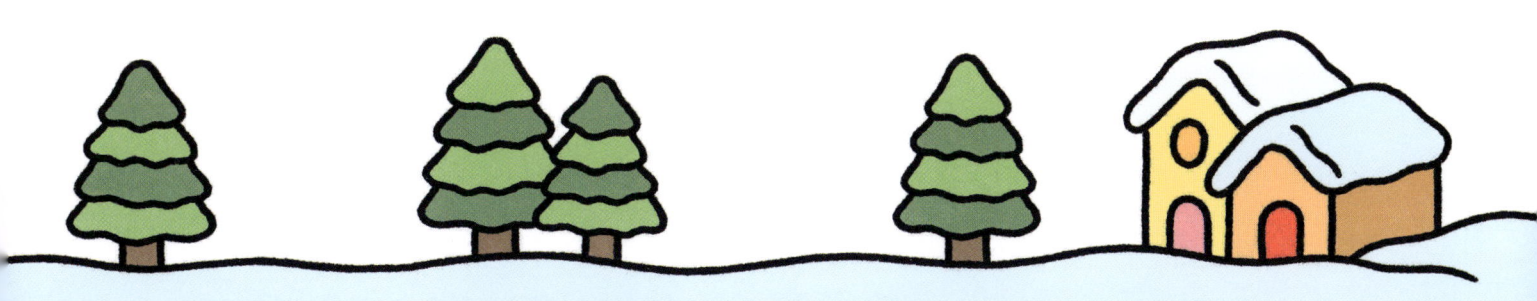

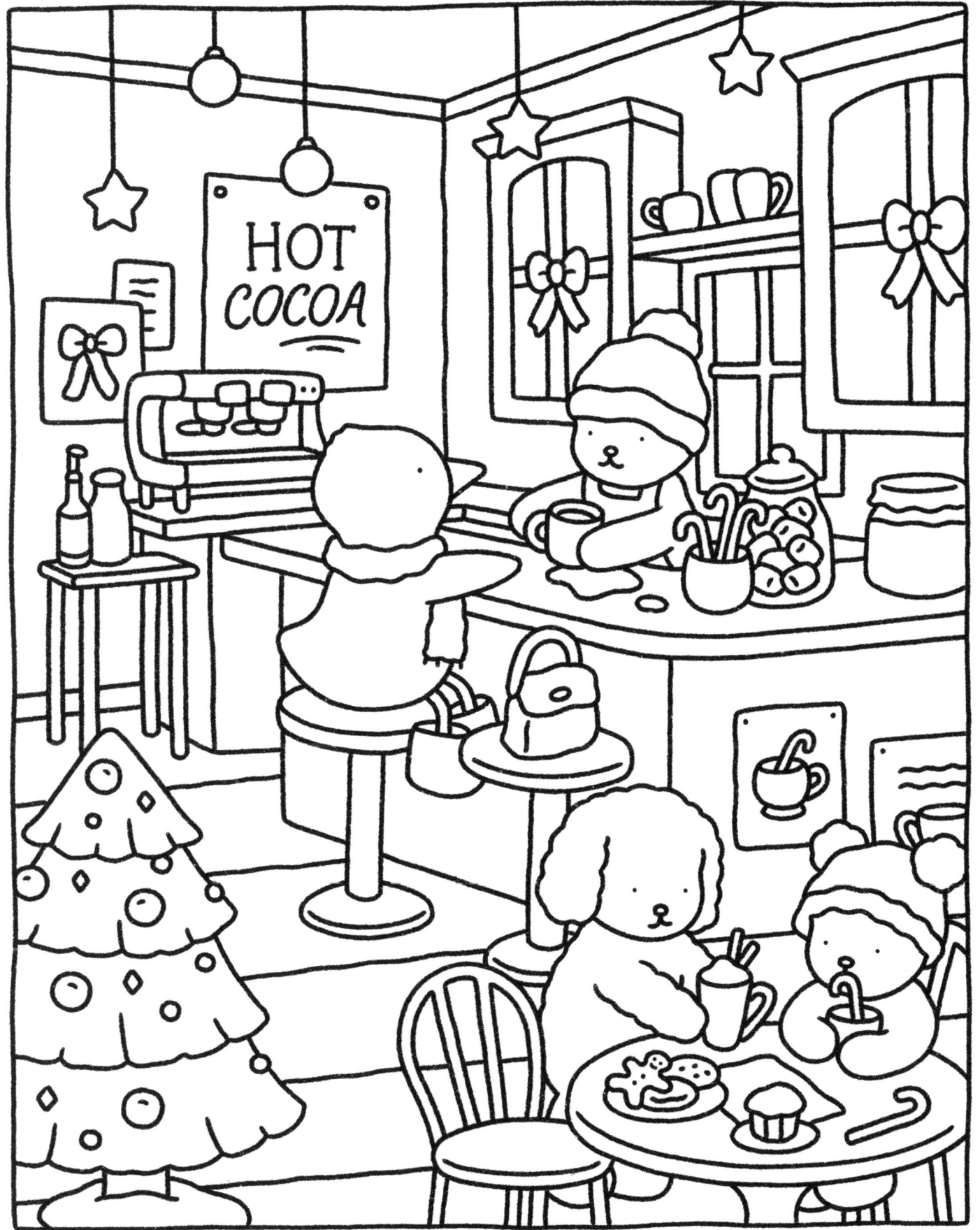

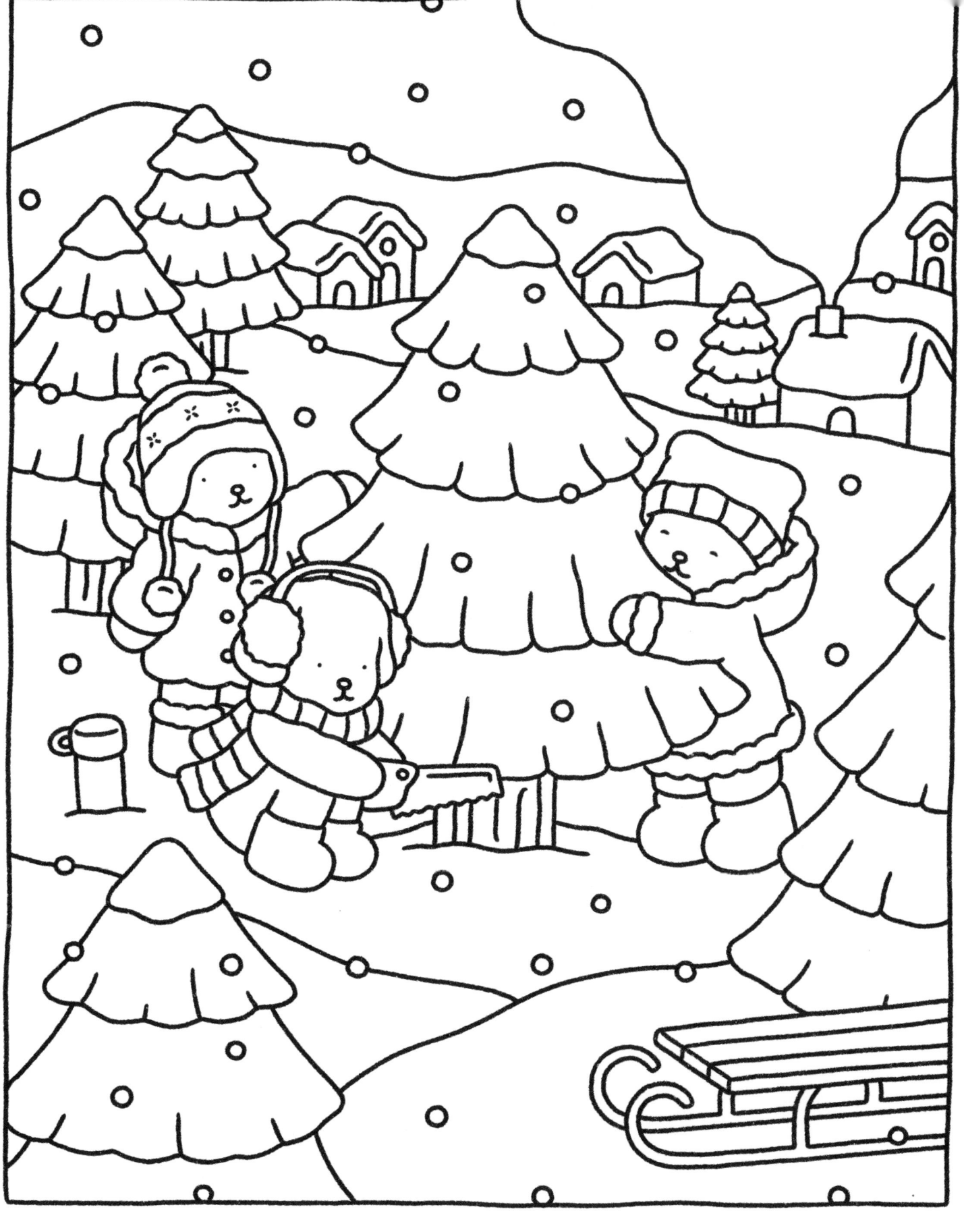

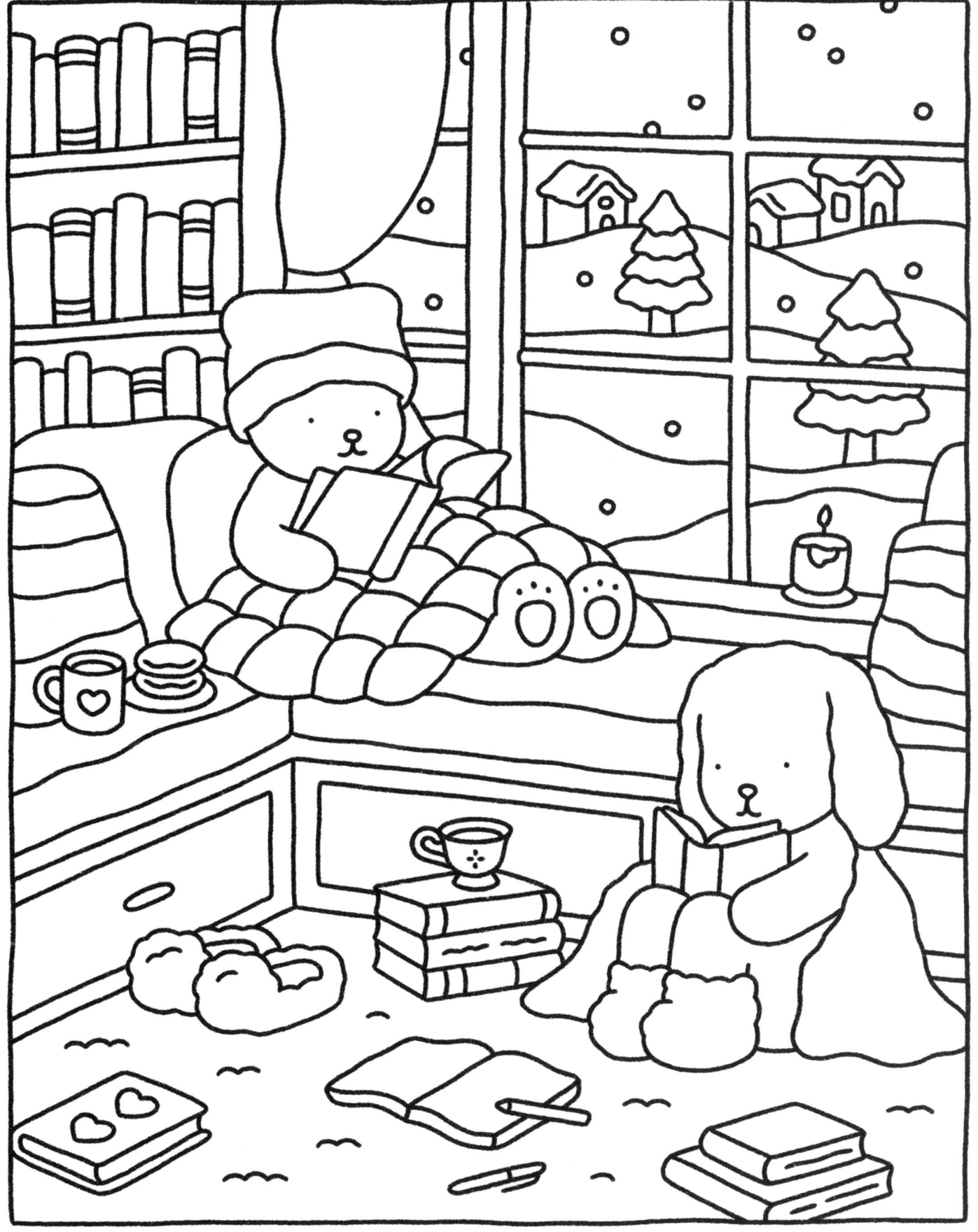

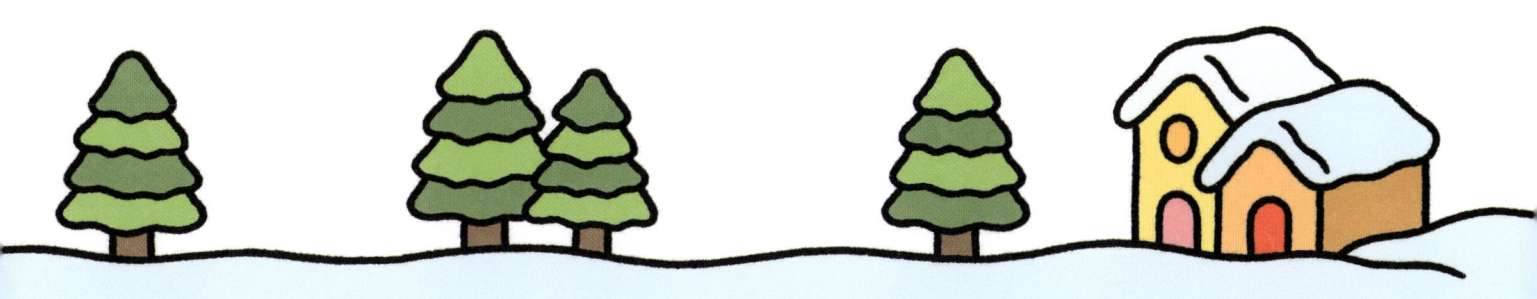

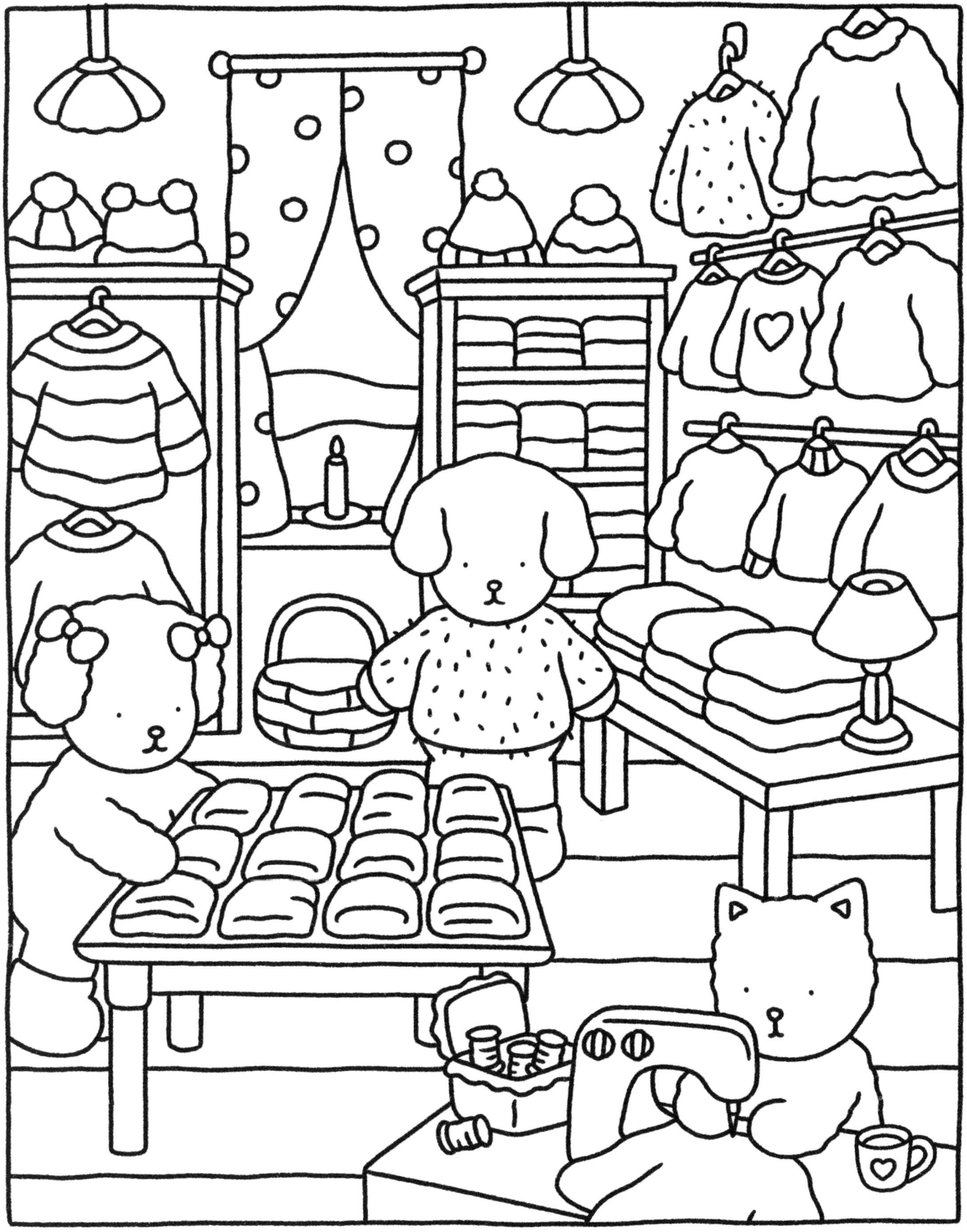

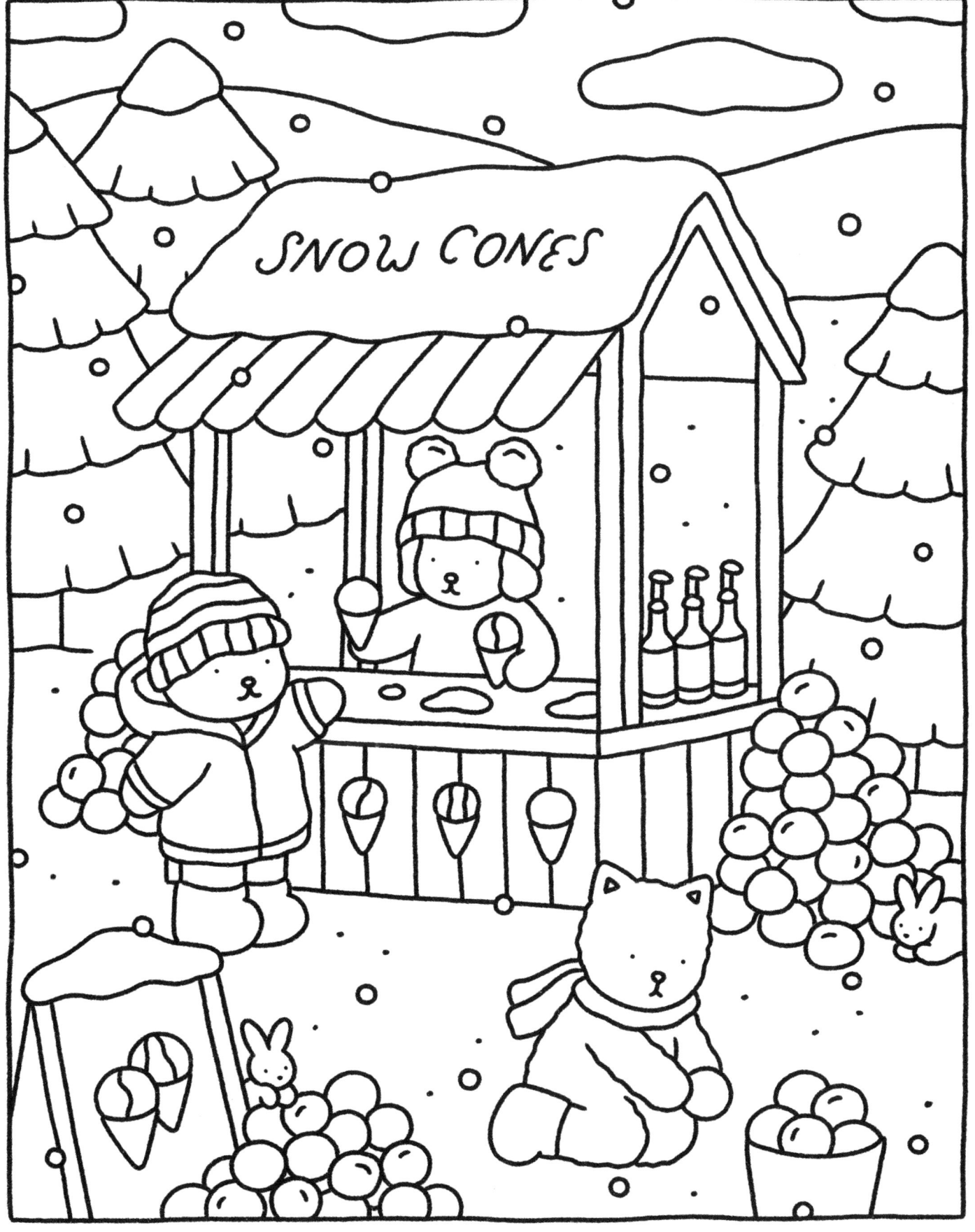